place photo here

These quotes belong to:

My Quotable Grandkid

A Grandparent's Journal of Unforgettable Quotes

CHRONICLE BOOKS

SAN FRANCISCO

ISBN 978-1-4521-2119-2

Manufactured in China

Design by Hillary Caudle

10 9 8 7

Chronicle Books LLC
680 Second Street
San Francisco, CA 94107

Chronicle Books publishes distinctive books and gifts.
From award-winning children's titles, bestselling cook-
books, and eclectic pop culture to acclaimed works
of art and design, stationery, and journals, we craft
publishing that's instantly recognizable for its spirit
and creativity. Enjoy our publishing and become part of
our community at www.chroniclebooks.com.

Quote ....
....
....
....
....
....
....
....
....
....
....
....
....
....
....
....
....
....
....

Who ....

Age ....

When ....

Where ....

....

Quote

....

....

....

....

....

....

....

....

....

....

....

Who ....

Age ....

When ....

Where ....

....

Who ....

Age ....

When ....

Where ....

....

Quote ....

....

....

....

....

....

....

....

....

....

....

....

....

....

Quote ....

....

....

....

....

Who ....

Age ....

When ....

Where ....

....

....

....

....

....

....

Who

Age

When

Where

....

Quote
....
....
....
....
....
....
....
....
....
....
....
....
....

Who ....

Age ....

When ....

Where ....

....

Quote ....

....

....

....

....

....

....

....

Quote

Who

Age

When

Where

Quote

....

....

....

....

....

....

Who ....

Age ....

When ....

Where ....

....

Quote

Who

Age

When

Where

Quote

....

....

....

....

....

....

....

....

....

                         ....

                         ....

                         ....

Who ....

Age ....

When ....

Where ....

....

Who

Age

When

Where

Quote

Who

Age

When

Where

Quote

Quote

....

....

....

....

....

....

Who ....

Age ....

When ....

Where ....

....

....

....

....

Quote

Who

Age

When

Where

Who ....

Age ....

When ....

Where ....

....

Quote ....

....

....

....

....

....

....

....

....

Quote

Who

Age

When

Where

Quote

....

....

....

....

....

....

....

....

....

....

....

....

....

....

....

....

Who

....

Age

....

When

....

Where

....

....

Quote

....

....

....

....

....

....

....

....

....

....

....

....

Who
....

Age
....

When
....

Where
....

....

Who

Age

When

Quote

Where

Quote ....

....

....

....

....

Who ....

Age ....

When ....

Where ....

....

....

....

....

....

....

....

....

Who

Age

When

Where

Quote

Who ....

Age ....

When ....

Where ....

....

Quote ....

....

....

....

....

....

....

....

....

Quote

....
....
....
....
....
....
....
....
....
....
....
....
....
....

Who

Age

When

Where

Quote

Who

Age

When

Where

Quote

....

....

....

....

....

....

....

Who ....

Age ....

When ....

Where ....

....

....

....

....

....

....

....

....

....

Quote

Who

Age

When

Where

Who ....

Age ....

When ....

Quote ....

Where ....

....

....

....

....

....

....

....

....

....

....

....

....

....

....

Who ....

Age ....

When .... Quote ....

Where ....

....

....

....

....

....

....

....

....

....

....

....

....

Quote

....

....

....

....

....

....

Who
....

Age
....

When
....

Where
....

....

....

....

....

Quote

....

....

....

....

....

....

....

....

....

....

....

....

Who ....

Age ....

When ....

Where ....

Who ....

Age ....

When ....

Where ....

....

Quote ....

....

....

....

....

....

....

....

....

Quote

Who

Age

When

Where

Quote

....

....

....

....

....

....

....

....

....

....

....

....

....

....

....

Who
....

Age
....

When
....

Where
....

....

Quote

....

....

....

....

....

....

....

....

....

                                    ....

                                    ....

                                    ....

Who
....

Age
....

When
....

Where
....

....

Who

Age

When

Where

Quote

Quote ....

....

....

....

....

Who ....

Age ....

When ....

Where ....

....

....

....

....

....

Who

Age

When

Where

Quote

Who ....

Age ....

When ....

Where ....

....

Quote ....

....

....

....

....

....

....

....

....

Quote

....
....
....
....
....
....
....
....
....
....
....
....

Who

Age

When

Where

Quote

....

....

....

....

....

....

....

Who

Age

When

Where

....

....

....

....

....

....

Quote

Who

Age

When

Where

Quote

....

....

....

....

....

....

....

....

....

....

....

Who

Age

When

Where

....

Who ....

Age ....

When ....

Where ....
....

Quote ....

....

....

....

....

....

....

....

....

....

....

....

....

....

....

Who ....

Age ....

When ....

Where ....

....

Quote ....

....

....

....

....

....

....

....

....

....

....

....

....

....

....

Quote

....

....

....

....

....

....

....

Who
....

Age
....

When
....

Where
....

....

....

....

....

Quote

Who

Age

When

Where

Who

Age

When

Where

Quote

Quote

....

....

....

....

....

....

....

Who ....

Age ....

When ....

Where ....

....

....

....

....

....

Quote

....

....

....

....

....

....

....

....

....

....

....

....

....

....

....

....

....

Who

....

Age

....

When

....

Where

....

....

Quote

....

....

....

....

....

....

....

....

....

                                        ....

                                    ....

                                ....

Who
....

Age
....

When
....

Where
....

....

Who ....

Age ....

When ....

Quote ....

Where ....

....

....

....

....

....

....

....

....

....

....

....

....

....

Quote

....

....

....

....

Who

....

Age

....

When

....

Where

....

....

....

....

....

....

....

Who ....

Age ....

When ....

Where ....

....

Quote ....

....

....

....

....

....

....

....

....

....

....

....

....

....

Who ....

Age ....

When ....

Where ....

....

Quote ....

....

....

....

....

....

....

....

Quote

Who

Age

When

Where

Quote

....

....

....

....

....

....

....

Who ....

Age ....

When ....

Where ....

....

....

....

....

....

Quote

Who

Age

When

Where

Quote

Who

Age

When

Where

Who ....

Age ....

When ....

Quote ....

Where ....

....

....

....

....

....

....

....

....

....

....

....

....

Who
....

Age
....

When
....

Where
....

....

Quote
....

....

....

....

....

....

....

....

....

....

....

....

....

....

Quote

....

....

....

....

....

....

....

Who

Age

When

Where

....

....

....

....

Quote

....
....
....
....
....
....
....
....
....
....
....
....

Who
....

Age
....

When
....

Where
....

Who ....

Age ....

When ....

Where ....

....

Quote ....

....

....

....

....

....

....

....

....

Quote

Who

Age

When

Where

Quote
....
....
....
....
....
....
....
....
....
....
....
....
....
....
....
....

Who
....

Age
....

When
....

Where
....

....

Quote

....

....

....

....

....

....

....

....

....

....

....

Who

....

Age

....

When

....

Where

....

Who ....

Age ....

When ....

Quote ....

Where ....

....

....

....

....

....

....

....

....

....

....

....

....

Quote ....

....

....

....

....

Who ....

Age ....

When ....

Where ....

....

....

....

....

....

Who ....

Age ....

When ....

Where ....

....

Quote ....

....

....

....

....

....

....

....

....

....

....

....

....

....

Who

Age

When

Where

Quote

Quote

....
....
....
....
....
....
....
....
....
....
....
....

Who
....

Age
....

When
....

Where
....

Quote

....
....
....
....
....
....

Who ....
Age ....
When ....
Where ....

....

Quote

....

....

....

....

....

....

....

Who

Age

When

Where

....

....

....

....

....

....

....

Quote

....

....

....

....

....

....

....

....

....

....

....

Who

Age

When

Where

....

Who ....

Age ....

When ....

Quote ....

Where ....

....

....

....

....

....

....

....

....

....

....

....

....

....

....

Who

Age

When

Where

Quote

Quote

....

....

....

....

....

....

....

Who

....

Age

....

When

....

Where

....

....

....

....

Quote

....

....

....

....

....

....

....

....

....

....

....

....

....

Who

Age

When

Where

Who ....

Age ....

When ....

Where ....

....

Quote ....

....

....

....

....

....

....

....

....

Quote ....

....

....

....

....

....

....

....

Who ....

Age ....

When ....

Where ....

....

....

....

....

....

Quote

....

....

....

....

....

....

Who
....

Age
....

When
....

Where
....

....

....

....

....

....

....

....

....

....

....

....

....

Quote

....

....

....

....

....

....

....

....

....

....

....

....

Who ....

Age ....

When ....

Where ....

....

Who

Age

When

Where

Quote

Quote ....
....
....
....
....
Who ....
Age ....
When ....
Where ....
....
....
....
....
....

Who ....

Age ....

When ....

Where ....

....

Quote ....

....

....

....

....

....

....

....

....

....

....

....

....

....

Who ....

Age ....

When ....

Where ....

....

Quote ....

....

....

....

....

....

....

....

Quote

Who

Age

When

Where

Quote

....

....

....

....

....

....

....

Who ....

Age ....

When ....

Where ....

....

Quote

....

....

....

....

....

....

....

....

....

....

....

....

....

....

Who

Age

When

Where

Quote

....

....

....

....

....

....

.... ,

....

....

....

....

....

Who

Age

When

Where

....

Who ....

Age ....

When ....

Where ....

....

Quote ....

....

....

....

....

....

....

....

....

....

....

....

....

....

Who

Age

When

Where

Quote

Quote

....

....

....

....

....

....

....

Who ....

Age ....

When ....

Where ....

....

....

....

....

Quote

Who

Age

When

Where

Who

Age

When

Where

Quote

Quote

Who

Age

When

Where

Quote

....

....

....

....

....

....

....

....

....

....

....

....

....

....

....

Who

....

Age

....

When

....

Where

....

....

Quote

....
....
....
....
....
....
....
....
....
                                        ....
                                        ....
                                        ....

Who ....
Age ....
When ....
Where ....

....

Who ....

Age ....

When ....

Quote .... Where ....

....

....

....

....

....

....

....

....

....

....

....

....

Quote ....

....

....

....

....

Who ....

Age ....

When ....

Where ....

....

....

....

....

....

....

....

....

Who

Age

When

Where

Quote

Who ....

Age ....

When ....

Where ....

....

Quote ....

....

....

....

....

....

....

....

Quote

Who

Age

When

Where

Quote

....

....

....

....

....

....

....

Who ....

Age ....

When ....

Where ....

....

....

....

....

....

Quote

....

....

....

....

....

....

....

....

....

....

....

....

....

....

Who

Age

When

Where

Quote

....

....

....

....

....

....

....

....

....

....

....

Who
....

Age
....

When
....

Where
....

....

Who ....

Age ....

When ....

Where ....

....

Quote ....

....

....

....

....

....

....

....

....

....

....

....

....

Who ....

Age ....

When ....

Where ....

....

Quote ....

....

....

....

....

....

....

....

....

....

....

....

....

....

Quote

....

....

....

....

....

....

....

Who ....

Age ....

When ....

Where ....

....

Quote

....

....

....

....

....

....

....

....

....

....

....

....

....

Who ....

Age ....

When ....

Where ....

Who ....

Age ....

When ....

Where ....

....

Quote ....

....

....

....

....

....

....

....

....

Quote

....
....
....
....
....
....
....

Who

Age

When

Where

....
....
....
....
....
....

Quote

....

....

....

....

....

....

....

....

....

....

....

....

....

....

....

Who

....

Age

....

When

....

Where

....

....

Quote

....
....
....
....
....
....
....
....
....
....
....
....

Who
....

Age
....

When
....

Where
....
....

Who ....

Age ....

When ....

Quote ....

Where ....

....

....

....

....

....

....

....

....

....

....

....

....

....

....

Quote ....
....
....
....
....
....
....
....
....
....

Who ....

Age ....

When ....

Where ....

....

Who

Age

When

Where

Quote

Who ....

Age ....

When ....

Where ....

....

Quote ....

....

....

....

....

....

....

....

....

Quote

....

....

....

....

....

....

....

....

....

....

....

....

Who
....

Age
....

When
....

Where
....

Quote

....

....

....

....

....

....

....

Who ....

Age ....

When ....

Where ....

....

....

....

....

....

Quote ....

....

....

....

....

....

....

....

....

....

....

....

....

....

....

....

Who ....

Age ....

When ....

Where ....

....

Quote

....

....

....

....

....

....

....

....

....

....

....

Who

Age

When

Where

Who ....

Age ....

When ....

Quote ....

Where ....

....

....

....

....

....

....

....

....

....

....

....

....

....

Who
....

Age
....

When
....

Where
....

....

Quote ....

....

....

....

....

....

....

....

....

....

....

....

....

Quote

....

....

....

....

....

....

....

Who ....

Age ....

When ....

Where ....

....

....

....

....

....

....

Quote

....

....

....

....

....

....

....

....

....

....

Who

Age

When

Where

Who . . . .

Age . . . .

When . . . .

Where . . . .

. . . .

Quote . . . .

. . . .

. . . .

. . . .

. . . .

. . . .

. . . .

. . . .

Quote

....

....

....

....

....

....

....

Who

Age

When

Where

....

....

....

....

....

....

....

....

Quote

....
....
....
....
....
....
....
....
....
....
....
....
....
....
....
....

Who
....

Age
....

When
....

Where
....

....

Quote

....

....

....

....

....

....

....

....

....

....

....

....

....

Who ....

Age ....

When ....

Where ....

....

Who ....

Age ....

When ....

Quote ....

Where ....

....

....

....

....

....

....

....

....

....

....

....

....

Quote ....
....
....
....
....

Who ....

Age ....

When ....

Where ....

....

....
....
....
....
....
....
....

Who

Age

When

Where

Quote

·······································

·······································

·······································

·······································

···

···

···

···

···

···

···

···

···

Who ....

Age ....

When ....

Where ....

....

Quote ....

....

....

....

....

....

....

....

....

Quote

....

....

....

....

....

....

....

....

....

....

....

....

Who

Age

When

Where

Quote

Who

Age

When

Where

Quote

....

....

....

....

....

....

....

....

Who

Age

When

Where

....

....

....

....

....

....

Quote

Who

Age

When

Where

Who ....

Age ....

When ....

Where ....

....

Quote ....

....

....

....

....

....

....

....

....

....

....

....

....

Who ....

Age ....

When ....

Where ....

....

Quote ....

....

....

....

....

....

....

....

....

....

....

....

....

....

Quote

....

....

....

....

....

....

....

....

....

....

....

....

Who

Age

When

Where

....

Quote

....

....

....

....

....

....

....

....

....

....

....

....

Who ....

Age ....

When ....

Where ....